Pheobe The Super Hero! Hero! Hero!

Copyright © 2020 by Neshele Godfrey

All rights reserved. No part of this book may be reproduced or transmitted in any form or by any means without written permission from the Author or Publisher.

Published by:

Ware Resources and Publishing

www.wareresources.com

1-888-469-4850 Ext. 2

ISBN 978-0-9974404-4-7

L.C.C.N: 2020900855

Printed in USA by Ware Resources and Publishing

Being a superhero is so hard I should know. I help lost kids get home, I save kids from bullies, I rescue small pets from trees, and I help our elderly cross the street. Even now, during the hottest month of the summer – scorching hot July! I wonder if anyone ever even notices. Sometimes I work without taking a lunch break. Imagine that citizens of Detroit why don't you. I save mothers, fathers, sisters, brothers, doctors, police, and children. If you're reading this book, then I probably saved you too!

I work so hard during the day that by the time I get home I'm completely exhausted. Too tired to help with the dishes, fight with my siblings, or listen to my parents. That doesn't stop my mom though. Every day without fail my mom always ask,

"Did you have a great adventure today? Was it hard work? Did you think of others before thinking of yourself? How many people did you help today sweetie pie?"

"Mommmmm, I don't know. I can't be bothered with all those details and that paperwork. I need a secretary, oh my Goddddd" I said glaringly.

Then I finally uttered the words,

"Do you want the job?"

A lightbulb goes off inside of my head. I began to remember that good help is hard to find these days. I should know because I overheard my dad yelling that to my brothers Jamar and Lamar last Saturday. My dad says, the only jobs that they would be good at was being lazy and hiding from work. They can never work for me. I'm hoping that my mom can do better. After all, she is Wonder Woman's mother.

After laughing for about five minutes straight, she handed me a package. Being that I love presents, I ripped the pink and blue wrapping paper right off in two tries. It was a red, white, and blue diary.

I looked at my mom frowning and said, "Mom, I'm not a little girl anymore. I'm a superhero fighting for our country. I don't have time to write in a baby's diary."

My mom explained, "It isn't a diary honey. That book is a Hero's Journal. I found it on eBay. Even Wonder Woman probably keeps a log too. You know, just in case a big producer wanted to write her biography."

I thought, why not. What can it hurt? Maybe someone will want to write my story. Someone like the great Queen Latifah. She can put it in a children's book. Or maybe a director like Spike Lee or John Singleton will make a screen movie about me. I can see it now. Billboards will read "Phoebe the Hero." People would see it for miles. The mayor would give me a key to the City of Detroit.

Better yet, The President would give me a light in the sky like Batman has. I can just see it now. Everyone will want to know who I am.

Who am I you asked? My name is Phoebe Sawyer age 8. My mom and dad own a home improvement business here in Detroit called Sawyer & Sons. I have 3 brothers and 1 sister: Jamar, Lamar, Kris, and Fonda. My family calls me Phoebe, but my friends call me "Wonder Woman."

That's right; you heard me. I am the new and improved Wonder Woman. No, I don't have an invisible helicopter. For now, I have a Schwinn 10-speed bike from Walmart.

After getting my bike on Christmas last year, my brother Kris and I decorated the entire bike with every Wonder Woman sticker that I could find in my toy chest. It's not an invisible airplane, but it works for now. And no, I don't have eye-catching Major Lee on speed dial. I would say that he's probably older than dirt right now. Probably the same age as Harriet Tubman or my mom. So, I replaced him with Thor.

Just in case you've been sleeping under a rock and don't know who Thor (Prince of Asgard) is; he is my future HUSBAND!

So, back off! Yeah, you heard me correctly. Thor and I are getting married as soon as I turn 21. My dad said 30 but I'm saying 21. We're going to live in Asgard too. I can't wait to decorate Asgard red, white, and blue.

"*Phoebe!*" my sister yells from downstairs.

"*Ugghhh!*" I replied. No matter how many times I tell them or ignore them, they refuse to conform. Since Phoebe is not my name, I yelled back, "*Sorry! There is no Phoebe here. But Wonder Woman is. Would you like her instead?*"

I heard another chuckle then my mom's voice, "Little Miss Wonder Woman, it's your turn to do the lunch dishes. So, come downstairs to wash the dishes right now young lady."

"*Mommmm!* I was on my way outside to wrap up for the night. Couldn't someone else do it?

"*No! Now come downstairs now!*" she replied sternly.

This family just doesn't get my job at all. I swear, being a superhero is hard work! That does it, now I'm mad. They don't know it, but they wouldn't like me when I'm mad. I can turn into the Incredible Hulk at any time when I'm mad.

With my bottom lip poking out, I entered the room of doom. How many people live in this house! I cannot believe it. There are so many dishes. You would think that our family owned a Ponderosa Restaurant instead of a home improvement company. The dishes reached from the bottom of the sink to top of the ceiling. I glance over the work ahead and of me and see the torpedo they left me. Jamar spilled Kool-Aid all over the table.

Lamar left the edges from his pizza on his plate. Miss Fancy Fonda left all her pepperoni toppings on her plate. If that weren't enough, Kris decided to leave a work of ketchup art on his plate. I felt the bubbling around my neck. I wondered if my skin was beginning to turn green. I huffed and I puffed. I even rolled my eyes a few times.

Before I knew it, I said it,

"That is it! My family is going to be the first entry in this hero journal. First page is going to read:

After what seemed to be 2 hours of hard labor, I was finally done. After getting permission, I sprinted out of the side door and I was off to the Madison Elementary School playground. I can't believe how late I am for work. I dash across our beautifully manicured green lawn.

Remembering how good it feels rubbing my feet back and forth on our soft sparkly grass. It always feels like a million tiny elves are massaging my feet. Mental note to self, make sure that I run barefoot across the grass again tonight.

I dash across my nosey neighbor Mrs. Shaw's lawn and I yelled,

"*Sorry about that Mrs. Shaw!*"

"*Stay off of my lawn!*" she yells back anyway.

Mrs. Shaw is always outside working on her lawn then sitting on her porch admiring her work. She says her lawn is going to win this year's best lawn contest. She must be close because every time she works on her yard my brothers just sit on our porch and stare at her. But that's another story for another day.

"Do you hear me Miss Phoebe?" she continued.

I swear, being a superhero is hard work. People just don't understand. We fight and save people's lives every day and all people ever thinks about it the details.

Luckily, our house is the second house off Grand River Road and in the heart of Rosedale Park. I was able to swiftly take a sharp left turn like I've seen Baltimore Ravens Randy Moss do. Then I did a little juke dance to throw off any incoming rivalries. I ran faster than the speed of light. Then I did a brief stop to gloat, make the ugliest frowning face, and busted the "Milly Rock" dance.

Hopefully, a big producer caught that dance groove. Then I took off running again. Two blocks later, I arrived at the playground. With the summer sun beaming on my face, I took a long look around the playground. I really love this park. Madison Park has seesaws, merry-go-rounds, a swing set, a slide, chin-up bars, a sandbox, and a baseball diamond. The grass was as green as ever.

Teenagers were listening to music and making murals on the far left of the park. In the kiddie corner, I see tons of small children and their parents playing carelessly. Some kids were eating ice cream and the rest were waiting patiently at the Ice Cream Stand. Over to the right, kids my age were having the time of their lives. Two known bullies were walking into the park with their little sister Angela.

I swear I just don't understand why Angela would ever want to hang out with the likes of them. Angela always tells everyone that her brothers are nice.

She says that they always make her lunch when she's hungry, plays with their Shih-Tzu dogs, and take her to the park. A few other people were playing tag and the remaining group were in a huddle. I quickly ran over to see what the big to do was about. Neighborhood kids Sierra and Colleen were selecting team players for a good game of dodgeball. Just in that moment, I caught a swing challenge in the corner of my eye. I quickly turn and made my way over there.

I jogged over to the empty swing and joined the race. The group of swingers had just started but I wasn't worried. I knew that I could catch up. I began stretching my legs out as far as they would go, then pulled them in tightly until I hit the bottom of my seat. I repeated this until I could feel myself being one with the swing. Every time the swing would start to travel downward, I would feel the jump in my stomach. It tickled me. It felt like I was touching the sun I was so high. Everyone began to cheer. I felt my smile coming on.

"Leave me alonnneeee!" Kris yelled.

I quickly scanned the playground to find him. He continued yelling. I looked behind him and could see those same two neighborhood bullies chasing him. Without a moment's thought I leaped off the swing. Luckily, I was already 6 feet in the air.

I spread my arms as I've seen Wonder Woman do a trillion times on the television.

"I got you little brother." I proclaimed.

Leave my brother alone!" I yelled to the boys.

Both boys stared at me like I was an alien that had just eaten their Thanksgiving dinner.

"Oh my God! Nate, do you see." One of them said.

"Aw man, I do. Let's get out of here before we get in trouble.

People are going to try to blame us for this."

The other one responded.

"Yeah! Get out of here!"

I yelled feeling accomplished.

Just then, a crowd started to form around us. With his eyes wide open, Kris stood up and held his hands over his mouth. He started shaking his head.

"Don't worry little brother. They won't bother you again, not while I'm around."

"Phoebe!" he screams.

"Who is she? Does anybody know where this little girl lives? Somebody please go get her mother!" a stranger yell.

My smile quickly leaves my face and I start to stare right back at the crowd. I slowly start standing up. A few people were whispering and pointing to my right arm. With my heart pounding, I slowly look down at myself.

Unknowingly to me, my right arm looked downright deformed. My poor arm was completely turned around.

"Ohhhh myyyy GODDDDD!" I yelled. Before I knew it, my heart start racing fast, and the tears came rushing through my eyes. I began crying uncontrollably.

Looking around I see a huge white boulder was sitting right next to me. Could it be true? Could I be human after all? Could it be that I flew into this huge boulder while saving Kris?

Someone in the crowd yelled that they knew where I lived and ran off. I'm sure that they were making their way to my house to inform my parents. My rescue was on its way.

All I had to do was hang in there until help arrived. I glance over to my brother who had begun to cry as well. Seeing my brother cry made me instantly brave. I didn't want him to be upset. After all, I am the big sister.

"Come here Kris. It's going to be alright. Don't cry. I promise I'm going to be okay. Daddy's going to fix my arm as soon as he gets here okay." I assured him.

"I'm so sorry you got hurt Phoebe…I mean Wonder Woman" he cried.

Just then, the crowd separated enough to allow my mom to enter.

"Are you okay Phoebe? Where does it hurt baby? Let mommy look at you?

"Mommmm" I said, "I'm fine. I just hit my arm. Dad can fix it when we get home."

"No baby. We must go to the hospital this time. Just to be on the safe side okay." My mom explained.

"Superheroes don't go to the hospital" I said sadly as tears ran down my face again.

I placed my left arm over my face to hide myself. I felt ashamed that I got hurt in front of all those people. All the while, I was thinking that my career was over.

We arrived at Children's Hospital. As we entered the emergency room, I looked around. I couldn't recall ever seeing so many sad and hurt people.

I couldn't help staring at everyone even though my mother repeatedly told me to stop. How could I have missed so many people needing my help? Just then, a little boy and his mother sat next to us.

"Hi" he said sadly,

"My name is Kwame Taylor. What's your name?"

"Wonder Woman"

I whispered.

"Like the superhero? Wow! I never met a superhero before"

he said cheering up.

"Live and in person but don't tell anyone okay"

I begged.

"Why not?" he asked curiously, "is it because you got hurt?"

I nodded.

"How did you get hurt? Did you catch the bad guys Wonder Woman?"

"Of course, I did Kwame. That's my job." I opened up. "Being a superhero is hard work, but someone has to do it. Today I just hit a huge boulder in the process. My mom is making me come her because my arm looks funny. See?"

I turned so that he can see my arm. As we started to compare injuries, a photographer from the Detroit Newspaper came up to us. He was tall, white, and had curly hair. He reminded me of Will Ferrell. I tried not to laugh. He took a good look at us and asked our parents if he could take our photos. Our parents agreed.

"Finally! Who are you with Spike Lee or John Singleton?" I asked.

"Well who are you little girl?" he asked.

Kwame interrupted, "Don't you know mister? Why that's Wonder Woman!"

"Wonder Woman huh!" he chuckled. "Well Wonder Woman, can I take your photograph?"

"Sure, you can. I thought you'd never ask!"

Right after that, my doctor called us into the room. Dr. Chan. Looked me over and said, "Well young lady, you are not Wonder Woman. It is not wise for you to take such risks. You have broken your arm and will need to take a break for eight weeks."

"Mom, can we go now? I protested.

My mom rolled her eyes at me and continued to listen to Dr. Chan's recommendations. According to know-it-all Dr. Chan, I couldn't be a superhero until my cast was removed. The nerve of that guy telling my mother that. I can feel my blood bubbling again. By the time we left the emergency room, I had a hard-white cast on my arm.

"I'm so sorry honey" My mom said, *"But I am so very proud of you today. You showed great courage helping your brother and here at the hospital. The world is such a better place with heroes like you are in it."*

"Thank you mom." I replied.

"You should put everything that happened today in your journal Wonder Woman. Maybe even make new plans for when the cast comes off. But no more rescues for a while."

"Maybe I will" I said matter-of-factly. *"Dr. Chan"* I whispered. That is it! Dr. Chan is going to be the second entry in this hero journal. Second page is going to read:

As we pulled up in front of our home, I remembered that I wanted to take a barefoot walk on our grass. I desperately needed those little soldiers to give me a foot massage now.

Looking at my mom's face, I know that's not going to happen tonight. All the kids on our block were standing in front of our house. This is just great, I thought to myself. Everyone is about to laugh at me. My siblings rushed over to help me get out of the car. All I could hear was everyone cheering for me. They had balloons and everything. Voices from everywhere screamed,

"Wonder Woman is home! Hooray!

As I looked around my yard I began smiling. They weren't looking at me like a failure. They were proud of me. I had done something good and they noticed. I guess I had my swagger back! Angela even found her way through the crowd. She whispered in my ear,

"My brothers said that they are very sorry you got hurt on the account of them. Phoebe do you accept their apology?"

"I guess" I moaned.

Just then, Mrs. Shaw came running across our grass to my mother. I know she only wanted the 411 on what happened to me. I softly whispered under my breath,

"Stay off my lawn Mrs. Shaw!"

The End!

About The Author

Neshele Godfrey is a poet, writer, and author of the new novel Phoebe the Super Hero. While Social Work and Human Services is her focus, community volunteering is her passion. She regularly provides free books throughout the Detroit Metropolitan Area.

WARERESOURCES AND PUBLISHING
WE ARE AN ALL IN ONE,
ONE STOP PUBLISHING COMPANY!!!!

W.R.P. is a modest but skillful and knowledgeable Christian Publishing Company. We specialize in getting authors into print. We embrace and guide each author like a member of our family. We treat you fairly and recognize the importance of building a lasting relationship with you as an author. Join us in the walk to promote prosperity along with the message of encouragement and peace. Be one of the authors we transform and prepare for the world of information and books.

FEEL FREE TO CONTACT US@
www.wareresources.com

1-800-469-4850 EXT. 2

Ware Resources and Publishing
You Start and Finish With Us!